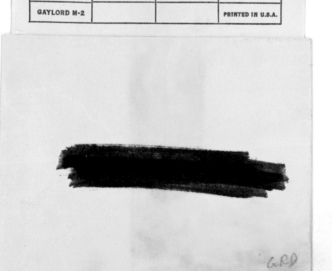

This Book Belongs
TO: _Vanessa Hoang_

_____

Come Along!

_____

Rebecca Caudill

COME ALONG!

Illustrated by Ellen Raskin

Holt, Rinehart and Winston

NEW YORK   CHICAGO   SAN FRANCISCO

By Rebecca Caudill

Come Along!
Contrary Jenkins
Did You Carry the Flag Today, Charley?
A Certain Small Shepherd
A Pocketful of Cricket
The Best-Loved Doll
Higgins and the Great Big Scare
Schoolroom in the Parlor
Saturday Cousins
Up and Down the River
Schoolhouse in the Woods
Happy Little Family

Text Copyright © 1969 by Rebecca Caudill.
Illustrations Copyright © 1969 by Ellen Raskin.
All rights reserved, including the right to reproduce
this book or portions thereof in any form.
Published simultaneously in Canada by Holt, Rinehart
and Winston of Canada, Limited.
SBN: 03-075425-9
Library of Congress Catalog Card Number: 69-11346
Printed in the United States of America
First Edition

For Ann Durell

because we share an Experience

Invitation

Come along, children!

    We'll roam meadow and mountain

And bring home treasure.

Spring is a poet,

    Chanting a lay of warm winds,

Swelling buds, and birds.

Two doves in a wood

    Coo softly to each other,

Celebrating spring.

Make haste! Run quickly

    To see my Easter garden.

A seed is risen!

Once I went to York.

　All that I remember is

A pear tree in bloom.

We lie in the grass,

    Our legs dangling in the stream,

And watch butterflies.

Patterns on a hill:

    Cattle grazing all one way,

Cloud shadows marching.

Who owns this meadow?

    Turtle, cricket, mole, and shrew.

I thought I owned it.

"Fling me a rainbow!"

I cry to the troubled sky,

And, look, she flings one.

This day I set apart—

It brought solitude, a thrush

At twilight, and you.

They utter no sound—

The midge, the beetle, the ant—

Yet I hear them sing.

We climb the long hill.

Daisies detain us, and moss,

And fiddlehead ferns.

The brown thrasher sings

  And dares me to be busy.

I stop and listen.

Forsythia blooms,

  And little winds of springtime

Ring the golden bells.

I catch a firefly

  In cupped hands. My fingers glow

With imprisoned fire.

We walk by the lake

　In the day's still evenglow.

A fish leaps in air.

Queen of the meadow

    Wears her purple crown and reigns

In the fall pasture.

Remember how we

    Ran to touch the touch-me-nots?

Yours sprang the farthest.

Reaper in the field,

    Did you not see the flowers

Nor the rabbit's nest?

On the autumn trail,

   Quiet, deep as longed-for peace,

Walks alongside me.

Saucy sassafras

   Decks itself in twelve gay hues,

And goes out clowning.

These you cannot buy:

   The scarlet of the sourwood,

The bronze of beeches.

Cold rain fell last night,

   Gold leaves today drip earthward,

And a lone bird sings.

I stare at the rain,

   And rain, like our old gray cat,

Stares coldly at me.

The day's lyric gift

   Was this: gray slanting raindrops

Against a stone wall.

The last sun-gold leaf

    Spins dizzily down to rest

Among the turnips.

Cows hunched in their stalls

    Wait the passing of winter

As they chew their cuds.

I hear ice breaking

    Among the branches of trees.

I kindle a fire.

28

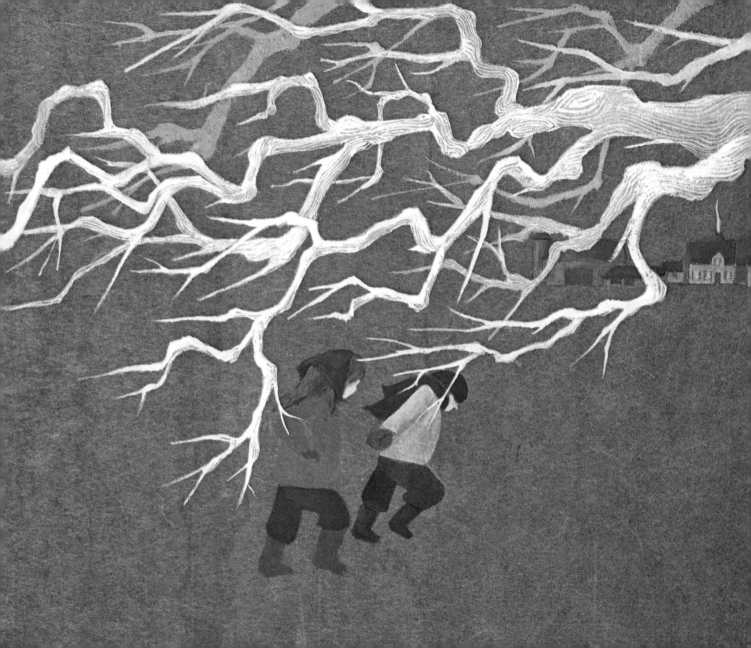

In dark December

    A flower blooms in the wood.

I think of Christmas.

We walk in starlight:

    Armies brandish gleaming swords

Of frost-jeweled grass.

About the Author: An accomplished author of books for young people, Rebecca Caudill has written some of today's best-loved stories for children, including *A Certain Small Shepherd, Did You Carry the Flag Today, Charley?* and 1965 Caldecott Medal runner-up *A Pocketful of Cricket.* Miss Caudill and her husband, James Ayars, with whom she wrote the tall tale *Contrary Jenkins,* live in Urbana, Illinois.

About the Artist: Ellen Raskin's work as illustrator and designer has brought her many awards, including the New York *Herald Tribune* Spring Book Festival Award for *Nothing Ever Happens on My Block* (1966), and the American Institute of Graphic Arts award for *Songs of Innocence* as one of the Fifty Books of the Year (1966). Author-illustrator of several children's books, Miss Raskin makes her home in New York City.

About the Book: Both the text and display type are set in Palatino. The book was printed by offset. The illustrations are best described by Miss Raskin herself: "I wanted the reader to see beyond the boundaries of the book as I tried to complement the author's word images with acrylic paint on colored rice paper. By not painting edge to edge, by avoiding an exact sense of scale or proportion, by eliminating shadows and horizons, I have hoped to achieve, not a picture of a landscape, but, like the haiku, a moment in nature."